Powerful Woman Tips

Also by this author

Reclaim Your Power, Reclaim Your Life: Living Your Life as a Powerful Woman

On the Path to Authentic Leadership: The OPAL Way to Leadership Success

Leading the Way in Diversity and Inclusion – Coaching Cards

Bringing Diversity and Inclusion to Life – Coaching Cards

Making Time – Part 3: The Juggle and the Struggle

with Mary Casey

From Diversity to Unity: Creating the Energy of Connection

with Catherine Brady

Are You Ready To Manage?

The Successful Manager

Getting To The Top

Powerful Woman Tips

100 Ways to Access and Live from Your Personal Power

Geraldine M Bown

© 2017 Geraldine M Bown.

All rights reserved.

This book or any portion thereof may not be reproduced or used in any manner whatsoever without the express written permission of the author.

Quotes from Is This Where I Was Going? by Natasha Josefowitz, and Samina Khan (www.fromthemudthelotus.com) reproduced with permission.

Edited and produced by Jessica Hopkins.

Cover design and layout by Nestor Michael.

Acknowledgements

With thanks to the thousands of women I have worked with over the years who have shown me the meaning of resilience, patience, compassion and humour.

Special thanks to my closest female friends who have supported me, made me laugh and reminded me of my own power in those moments when I forgot.

Greatest thanks and appreciation to my daughters Lucy and Jessica who I am sure I neglected at times when I was working to help women! You have become amazing, powerful women in your own right. May you continue to inspire all the women you meet to find and live from their power, as you are doing. I love you both enormously.

Special mention and thanks to my daughter Jessica who has edited this and my other latest books and overseen the publication process for me.

Welcome to Powerful Woman Tips

The Powerful Woman Tips were first created as a weekly email. There are 100 unique tips – almost two years' worth of weekly emails. Now they are together in one place so you have a handy reference to guide you on your journey to becoming more powerful.

Let this be your at-hand source for short, practical and easy to read tips and insights that will help you to sustain inner balance, be more visible and valued at work and direct your life from a more powerful place. In short – transform how you live your life.

And before you think that being powerful doesn't apply to you because you are not a senior manager somewhere… I'm talking about *inner power.* The power that is already in you and waiting to be expressed in a beautiful, fulfilling life.

Do you ever find yourself thinking:

- *There's nothing I can do about my situation. I just have to bite the bullet and get through it.*
- *The only way to reduce guilt is to do more: more at work and more at home.*
- *If anyone has to suffer it will have to be me. So I'll just forget about getting my own needs met and make sure everyone else is OK.*

Well this book is specifically for you because there *is* a way you can see your situation entirely differently. And I don't mean a fleeting change that works for a couple of days before you slide back into the old way of thinking.

We all need a little help and guidance at times in our lives. So I have put together these Tips to help you make some changes and sustain them.

They cover topics such as dealing with stress, dealing with children, dealing with a difficult boss, dealing with a difficult situation, dealing with stereotypical comments and many more.

Keep this book handy and know that whatever is going on in your life, there is probably a Tip to help you through it.

And welcome to the new powerful you.

Enjoy!

Geraldine

How to use this book

Each Tip has one key idea and one action so they are easy to remember and easy to implement. Although some of them you need to implement again and again until they become natural to you.

There are a number of ways you can use this book:

1. Read one Tip every week (or even every day) and focus on that for the whole week.
2. Read through the Tip headlines and see which resonates with you today, right now, and focus on that for a week.
3. Pick a page at random knowing that it must be the message you need today!

Or pick and choose depending on how you feel. It's a resource to use in multiple ways, time and again, for as long as you need.

The Powerful Woman Tips

1. Learn to appreciate yourself
2. Never be interrupted again
3. How to empower your children
4. Face forward when things go wrong
5. Create the lead role of your life
6. Keep hold of your power in stressful situations
7. Learn how to say no
8. Getting your needs met
9. Get noticed at work to advance
10. Let your heart guide you
11. Being strong doesn't mean being silent
12. You have earned your position
13. You don't have to do it alone
14. You have a right to be included
15. Resist female gender roles
16. Stop saying sorry
17. Be a dolphin, not a shark
18. Choose where you put your energy
19. Are you making up stories about others?
20. Be more effective in meetings
21. Integrate the masculine and feminine
22. There are no wrong decisions
23. Teach yourself confidence
24. The difference between explaining and justifying
25. Managing friendships on social media
26. It's OK for people to not like you
27. There is more than one way to listen
28. Accept and embrace compliments
29. Just because you're good at it, doesn't mean you should do it

30. Rethink how you see success and failure
31. You're the only expert you'll ever really need
32. Don't make *their* pain *your* pain
33. Change your experience of yourself
34. Let courage trump fear
35. It's OK to show your vulnerability
36. Is a weakness actually a strength?
37. Don't rush to restore order to chaos
38. Don't be defensive
39. Not everything worth doing is worth doing well
40. Put yourself first sometimes
41. Don't keep quiet about what you want
42. Turn negatives into positives
43. *Everyone* is responsible for running a smooth household
44. Which qualities are you wearing today?
45. The balance you *can* achieve
46. Make time for appreciation and gratitude
47. You are more powerful than you know
48. Question the voice that says 'I'm not ready yet'
49. Dealing with advice
50. Update your support network
51. Take a moment to take stock
52. Are you happy with who you are?
53. Focus on what you *have* done
54. Be aware of hidden opportunities
55. The connection between passion and persuasion
56. Sometimes it's good to rock the boat
57. Reject the myth that women aren't good at networking
58. It's time to give yourself a break
59. You are *not* an impostor
60. Countering workplace myths

61. Why you need a mentor *and* a sponsor
62. It's your right to ask for what you want
63. Comparisons kill confidence
64. Don't deflect credit for *your* hard work
65. Equal treatment doesn't mean same treatment
66. The fine line between comfortable and complacent
67. Don't give away your personal power
68. You can use your power without abusing your power
69. What's love got to do with it?
70. Developing your personal power is a lifetime's work
71. Goals are good; intent is better
72. A better way to approach presentations
73. You have the power to change your life
74. One size doesn't fit all
75. The only time to consider what you wear
76. It's not just about the job
77. Your body is your friend
78. The importance of building relationships in your career
79. Being assertive is not being aggressive
80. Let's practise detachment
81. A new way of looking at your job
82. Keep your energy high
83. The head vs. the heart
84. Acknowledge the truth about yourself
85. Change your self-talk
86. The perfection block
87. The importance of knowing yourself
88. How to fail
89. Taking risks takes practice
90. Redefining luck
91. The 4D approach to household tasks
92. Choose your body language carefully

93. Your relationship with yourself
94. Are you willing to change?
95. Warriors offer peace first
96. The importance of looking after your body
97. The important meeting is the one *before* the meeting
98. Myths about delegating at home
99. How to develop a personal vision
100. The golden rules for every busy woman

1

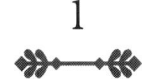

Learn to appreciate yourself

Think about what is great about *you*. How you behave and relate to others will be affected by how you think about yourself, so it's important to reinforce and maintain a positive self-image at all times.

Write down five things you really like about yourself on a piece of paper. You can consider anything – particular skills or strengths you have; something about your appearance you like; your positive personality attributes. Draw from all areas of your life: home, work and social.

Once you have your five written down, put the piece of paper next to your bed. Look at them before you go to sleep and again when you wake up. Take delight in what is great about you. Remember them especially when you have a bad day, or if someone says something hurtful to you – they will give you strength.

**Concentrate on the brilliance that is YOU.
Take delight in and celebrate yourself.**

2

Never be interrupted again

It's a personal right to express your opinions and values and have them listened to. That includes disagreeing with others and refusing to be put down, interrupted or ignored.

If someone starts to interrupt you say, 'I would like to finish what I was saying' and at the same time put up your hand in a "stop" position at about waist height. It will stop them talking. Then continue with your point. Don't pause otherwise they will continue with their interruption. When you have finished your point you can then turn the person and say, 'Now what was it that you wanted to say?'

This takes practice to implement but is a valuable and important step on your way to becoming a powerful woman.

Make sure you are heard.

3

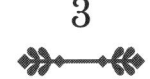

How to empower your children

Women have so many things do deal with, to take care of, to be responsible for, that sometimes we forget that we have the lead role in the movie of our lives. Right now maybe we can't change the script: we can't magic a new boss, or stop the baby teething, or take our parents' ailments away. But we can change how we act out the script, and how we live our lives.

One of the ways we can do this is to look at the small community of people we live with – our family. I think the best service we can give our children is to teach them to be responsible for their own little lives and I don't think they are ever too young to start.

Let's look at remembering things for school as an example. My daughters might say, 'We're going on a field trip on Thursday and will need our boots.' So I would say, 'OK. Well you need to make sure you remember then. Write it on a sticky note and put it over your bed or on your bedroom door so you don't forget.'

You can elaborate by saying, 'Each day I have my own things to remember and I might not be able to remember all of yours as well. But, if you use a sticky note, then you can be sure you'll remember everything you need.' Give them the opportunity to start organising their own lives.

It's the beginning of getting children to be personally responsible. You don't need to do it for them if they are capable of doing it for themselves.

Encourage your children to be more responsible for themselves.

4

Face forward when things go wrong

The easiest thing to do when something goes wrong is to make it someone else's fault and blame them. This way we can stay in anger and self-righteousness and feel justified in giving vent to our bad feelings.

The problem with this thinking is that it paralyses us. Of course things go wrong in our lives sometimes and we get disappointed, hurt and angry. But we're not supposed to stay there, and nor do we have to.

Nothing will change what has already happened so we need to assess what we want to do now. How can we respond positively? What do we need to do to make things better? We have a choice in how we respond, both practically and emotionally. As soon as we move into that mode our power will begin to flow and we start taking charge of our lives again.

Move out of blame and make new choices.

5

Create the lead role of your life

This is *your* life and you are playing the lead. Not only that, you get to be the scriptwriter as well. And what's more, you are the director of it all too. How good is that!

So decide on the characteristics for your character – strong, assertive, determined, honest, competent, inspirational… and then start to act in role.

When people try to put you down and write a different character, remind yourself that they are not in charge of your script – *you* are! Rip up their script, don't learn their lines and don't act like the person they have made up.

You have the final say so play to your strengths and play to your power.

Write your role. Act your role. Live your role, and lead your life.

6

Keep hold of your power in stressful situations

It's very tempting, and easy, to be drawn into someone's emotional turmoil when they attack you verbally – especially if you feel their anger is misplaced.

When we are attacked we want to defend ourselves and often we want to attack back. But as soon as you become embroiled in someone's negative emotion cycle, you are getting on their wheel and going nowhere.

If you allow others to dictate how and where you respond you are giving them your power on a plate. Stay calm. Don't engage with people at this level.

You can decide how you are going to respond to what they have said, and you can choose when and where. See each time it happens as another opportunity to practise a measured approach to an attack.

Respond to others' outbursts on your terms.

7

Learn how to say no

This is hard when we have been brought up not to disappoint people. And hard when we think that saying no means we reject someone (because sometimes when someone says no to us *we* feel rejected).

When we say no we are refusing a request – not rejecting a person. If someone asks you to do something you don't want to do but you find yourself about to agree, buy yourself some time and say, 'Let me think about that and get back to you.' You can then work out how you can refuse the request.

Every time you agree to do something you don't want to, and then resent it or feel like a martyr, you give away a little bit of your power – to other people. You need your power with you, inside you, all the time.

Say no to the things you really don't want to do.

8

Getting your needs met

You have a personal right to express your needs and have them listened to. Unfortunately, we are usually far more concerned about meeting other people's needs than having our own met, so aren't very good about accepting, or claiming, this right.

First you have to decide *what* you need (I need more time for myself; I need more help in the house; I need to be included in that meeting). Then you have to *tell* whoever needs to hear. Ask yourself if this is easier to do at work or at home? You need to be able to do it in both places. And the only way is practise, practise, practise.

Choose two needs you have right now – one at home and one at work – and state your needs to the people who need to hear them this week. The more you hear yourself voicing your needs the more confident you will be about doing it.

Start to vocalise your needs.

9

Get noticed at work to advance

Put simply, if you want to advance at work you have to use your initiative, trust your judgement, and apply it to decisions that are within your area of control. Don't look constantly to other people for help and reassurance or to make decisions for you. You need to be looking for ways to demonstrate that you are competent and ambitious.

Two ways to help you to get noticed at work:

Offer to do some of your manager's tasks.
Show that you are keen to improve your abilities and would regard any delegation from your manager as a new challenge.

Ask for extra responsibility.
If you feel that you can handle a particular task you are not doing at the moment then put yourself forward for it.

Don't be afraid to take some risks. People don't grow if they don't take risks. For some women the fear of failure is greater than the desire for success. But in order to succeed you need to put your initiative to use and be excited for what that might bring – whether that be success *or* failure.

Be more visible at work and be ready to learn, whatever the outcome may be.

10

Let your heart guide you

Engaging the heart as well as the head is a powerful combination. Your integrity lives in your heart, and integrity is both the ability to do the right thing and the ability to know what the right thing to do is.

In our working environments we see situations every day where people compromise who they are. They don't give voice to their most creative ideas. They withhold their most deeply held feeling or most cherished aspirations because they feel the environment is not safe and that it won't support such unique aspects of them. And often this is true: our working environments aren't safe a lot of the time.

Whenever we reveal our true selves and act in ways that are not the norm of those around us, we subject ourselves to the possibility of ridicule, judgement and, even worse, out-and-out retaliation.

However, this is all in the ego's world. A world full of competition, attack and defence. We are always going to be the object of someone else's desire for control, or their manipulation for getting their own way. When people act in these ways, it is simply because they are operating from the ego and not from the heart. They are not operating from a place of compassion and love.

Listening to your heart means that you will be guided to act in ways that are not about playing ego games. You will receive clear guidance and you will have the courage to act on your insights and remain in your integrity.

How many of us have gone along with something at work even though we felt it was a wrong decision or, at the very least, made us feel uncomfortable? How many of us stay silent when a sexist joke is made or when someone is ridiculed or humiliated? Or when a decision is made that we don't agree with?

It takes great courage to step forward and say, 'I feel very uncomfortable about this,' but having the courage to act with integrity can inspire others to do the same.

Organisations will only change when the quality of everyone's interactions changes. And by learning to create a link between our hearts and our heads, we stay in touch with what is true and integral to us. That heart/head line where courage and integrity lie will take us right to our inner power – as well as our inner peace.

Find your integrity in your heart – then act from it.

11

Being strong doesn't mean being silent

Women have amazing inner strength. Organising the household; sorting out family relationship problems; contributing to the local community… not to mention our paid job. Managing all these strands means we have built up tremendous inner resources, strength and energy, which is good news because we need it!

But we must make sure we don't pay the price for being a strong woman. Tip 8 looks at asking for what you need. So what price might you pay if you don't ask for help?

Because people see you as strong, they might see you as coping and not needing help. When my daughters were aged 6 and 3, and I was setting up my business, my mother-in-law was diagnosed with cancer. She and my father-in-law came to live with us for six months and she died with us. She saw me as her main support. It was an incredibly stressful time.

I could have really used help from my friends – from the women I had helped when they were stressed; from those I had given my time to when they needed support. But they were nowhere to be seen and I felt incredibly let down. Some time later I talked to them about this. They said that I seemed to be coping so well they didn't realise I needed help. They also said, 'So why didn't you ask us to help?' They were right and I learned a very important lesson: if you don't tell people you need help then you won't get it. It's great to be strong – but it's also a sign of strength to ask for what we need and say how we feel, not a sign of weakness.

Always ask for help when you need it.

12

You have earned your position

When you move higher up the scale, it may well be that there will be fewer women around you. In a traditionally male environment being the token woman can garner insinuations that you only got the job *because* you are a woman. So how do you counter these?

Unfortunately there will always be people who will say that and the tiny minority at the end of the scale who are prepared to be antagonistic to you are unlikely to change no matter what you do. Don't waste your time trying to change them, but equally, do not tolerate rude or uncooperative behaviour.

Here are some options of dealing with negative reactions and comments:

In answer to the comment, 'You would say that, you're a woman.'
Say, 'I am not speaking on behalf of all of womankind, I am speaking for myself.'

Address the comments openly at a team meeting.
Say you don't appreciate their comments and you expect the highest performance from your team and they can expect the same from you.

Ignore the comments.
Have faith that you will win people round with your commitment, leadership style, and your results.

You've worked hard to get to where you are: you know you deserve it.

**Recognise your own competence
and ability to do the job – and own it.**

13

You don't have to do it alone

The higher you go, the fewer women there are – for the time being at least – and that can sometimes create a feeling of isolation. You look around you and there are no other women at your level. There's nothing wrong with the guys – you like working with men. But you are starting to feel a bit like the odd one out.

This is where women's networking really comes into its own. There are many women at your level of seniority. Women with similar skills and talents who see the world through similar lenses and whose brains work in similar ways. They may be in the same industry – they just don't necessarily work in your organisation.

You have to find out where they are. Check out online and offline networks. For example, there is likely to be a network in your professional association or you can join the local Chamber of Commerce (UK) and attend their meetings. Consider both these global networks: The Women's Executive Network WXN (wxnetwork.com) or PWN the Professional Women's Network (pwnglobal.net). Talk to women like you who have similar concerns and approaches. It's not that you're looking for agreement on everything. It's just that you want to feel you are in a territory where you can speak and understand the language.

Of course we need to be careful about polarisation between the genders. But there are male/female differences that we would be foolish to ignore, and you need support now, which means you need to find women who can support you.

Once there are equal numbers of men and women at senior levels you will have lots of choice about finding kindred spirits. Until then, you might need to go further afield to find them. And once you do, you'll feel relief, get invaluable support and make great contacts.

Join a women's network today.

14

You have a right to be included

You know the joke about decisions being made in the men's room and on the golf course… well it's not always a joke. Don't want to play squash at lunch or go to the bar on a Friday after work? Then unfortunately that means you might be excluded.

Men won't be doing these things intentionally in order to deliberately exclude you. But if you choose not to go then there's a good change that you won't be involved in important discussions.

Don't allow yourself to be excluded. Set up some social occasions that everyone can enjoy – you won't be the only one being excluded.

Every organisation is committed to Inclusion so bring it up and look at how it is being implemented. Make the unconscious conscious then everyone can see the whole picture.

You could ask: 'Might there be a diversity/inclusion issue we are missing here?' Or tackle specific issues: 'Do we always have to meet after work? This excludes people who have childcare responsibilities. Can we meet at a lunchtime?' Or: 'I think some women might feel excluded from this. Why don't we…'

You are doing it to raise awareness not to beat people over the head. But stay in the mix – stay in the conversation.

Keep yourself at the heart of decision-making.

15

Resist female gender roles

Are you expected to be the one who pours the coffee? Takes the minutes? (Yes, it does still happen.) And is it being petty and churlish to object?

No. And you must object, but in the right way. Because – whether you like it or not – you are a role model for women and I believe all women have a responsibility to the women coming up behind them to make things better. So if something needs to change then so much the better that it's you who helps to bring that change about.

Changing people's stereotypical assumptions is a slow process of raising their awareness every time the stereotype shows itself. And there are effective but non-threatening ways to do it.

If you are expected to pour the coffee say, 'I'm happy to pour the coffee today because it will be a while then before it's my turn again.' And then make sure you don't pour again until others have taken a turn. Re the minutes you could say, 'Is there a volunteer to take the minutes or shall we take it in turns?'

You don't need to make a point about what you are *not* prepared to do and why – just suggest how you want it to work and then act accordingly.

Set a positive example and challenge female gender roles where you can.

16

Stop saying sorry

Of course it's important that if you *are* sorry you say so, but it's amazing how many women overuse that word.

We say sorry when we want to start a conversation; we say sorry if someone disagrees with us; we even say sorry when someone bumps into *us*! Using the word sorry inappropriately, and frequently, puts you in a position of "less than", giving the message that we are sorry we even exist.

Monitor yourself for a week by eliminating the word altogether. If you are genuinely sorry about something use a word like regrettably or unfortunately. By resolving not to use the word sorry at all, you will easily see just how many times you are tempted to say it.

Only say sorry when you genuinely are.

17

Be a dolphin, not a shark

It's difficult to swim with the sharks without becoming one. Some women deliberately adopt the male characteristics they see being rewarded and resolve to change when they reach a position of real power. But it's stressful to try and live like a shark if you're really a dolphin.

Every organisation says they want their people to bring their whole selves to work. Women have a great opportunity to bring forth their inner power and resources, their gifts and perspectives and contribute to a new kind of leadership, which is sorely needed in our organisations.

To do this you need to be able to tap into your authentic self and have the courage not to compromise your personal values. There are women in very senior positions in organisations already doing this. Find out who they are and what they do. Use them as your role models. Ask one of them to mentor you.

Your feminine power is really needed. Stay true to yourself and become more of who you are. That is how you will make your mark and help to create the organisations that every employee is dreaming of.

Embrace – and act from – your feminine power.

18

Choose where you put your energy

Powerful women are mindful where they put their energy. Energy follows thought. What we think about expands. Think about it: when you are considering buying a particular make of car, you start noticing that car everywhere you go.

Many people have used a vision board to good effect – they find photos of the things they want, put them on a board, think about them and look at them daily. They testify to getting the things they want more quickly through doing this.

But beware: if all we think about is wanting – wanting a better job, wanting more money – then it's *that* what we will get more of; the wanting of it! Using thoughts positively can bring great benefits. But it also works with negative thoughts. Are you still complaining about something that happened last week? Still angry about what that person said? Don't keep talking about the bad stuff – you'll keep it alive.

Don't leave your spirit (and your power) back there: you need it *here*, now, inside of you, so you can live the full life that's right in front of you. Think about which thoughts are directing your energy. Thousands of thoughts come into our heads daily – you don't have to believe them all.

Keep your focus on positive thoughts.

19

Are you making up stories about others?

Everyone loves a story and we love listening to great storytellers. But what about the stories we make up about other people? We can often do this without realising that's what we are doing and what's more we believe them and then act as if they are true.

We start to run stories about people almost as soon as we meet them. We look at someone's face, or clothes, or tattoos, or jewellery, or *anything,* then we find ourselves thinking, 'Oh they're probably...' or, 'I bet they're...' And then we look for evidence that we were right – about the story we just made up!

Don't believe the thoughts you have about others, especially if that thought leads you to think badly of them, or worse, treat them badly. Try to notice when you do this and consciously stop your assumptions and judgements.

Check the assumptions you make about others.

20

Be more effective in meetings

The higher up the ladder you go the more time you will spend in meetings, so it's important to be effective.

Here are two ways you can be more effective:

Always make a contribution.
If you are new to your post and feel that you don't know enough yet to contribute (this won't actually be true because you will have been invited to the meeting *because* you have something to contribute) then, at the very least, make a comment about someone else's contribution: 'I agree with Jean's point...' or, 'I think Sam made an important point when he said...' Not only will this help your relationships with your colleagues, but your voice will also be heard.

Ask for a response.
If you do make a contribution and you don't get much response then ask for one. For example, you could say: 'I'd love to know what you think about...' Or: 'I'd love some feedback on my idea.'

Never leave a meeting not knowing what people thought about what you said.

> **Make sure your voice is heard in every meeting you attend.**

21

Integrate the masculine and feminine

We are used to hearing about masculine qualities as being directive, forceful, autocratic, controlling and feminine qualities as being co-operative, empathetic, and listening. While it may be true that, generally, masculine qualities are evidenced more in men and feminine qualities more in women, that obscures the point.

Yes, we need a better balance of masculine and feminine qualities in organisations but integrating the masculine and feminine has nothing to do with men and women. It's the marriage that has to take place within ourselves. We all have to develop masculine and feminine qualities. We can then decide which of these qualities are appropriate for the situation.

This is good news for women. Having seen many masculine qualities rewarded in organisations, many women have already learned them. But we mustn't deny or lose access to our feminine qualities in the process. It is only when men and women have access to their own masculine and feminine that we can really start to talk about equality.

Access your masculine and feminine qualities, and use them all appropriately.

22

There are no wrong decisions

We've all made decisions we question in hindsight. But you must remember that there is no such thing as a wrong decision. We make decisions based on the best information we have in the moment. If we had known better at the time we would have chosen differently, right?

We can, however, make *another* decision whenever we get new information or a new insight, whether that's 10 minutes, 10 days, 10 weeks, 10 months or 10 years after we first made a decision.

So we choose. Then we choose again. And again. And again. The mistake would be to live with a decision instead of choosing again and making another decision. It's not about changing your mind – it's about making another decision. There are no wrong decisions: there are only new choices.

Be ready and willing to act on new insights.

23

Teach yourself confidence

Why do so many competent, amazing women have no confidence in themselves? Of course there are many reasons why this might be the case but let's concentrate on what can we do about it.

It would help for you to define exactly what confidence looks like to you. What do self-confident people do that you don't do? What do they say that you don't say? How do they stand? How do they walk? How would you be different if you had more self-confidence?

Write a complete list entitled, *'As a confident woman I...'* Make sure you write in the present tense and make it as long as you like. Then take each line one by one to focus on and work at. Take two or three things a week, or more once you get going. The more you adopt confident behaviours, the more people will relate to you as being confident and the more confident you will feel. It's just practice!

Act confident to become confident.

24

The difference between explaining and justifying

Sometimes we think we are explaining but people give us feedback that we were justifying. So what's the difference?

The difference is in *how* you explain. If there is any trace of guilt when you explain then it becomes justification, and you will sound like you are desperate to convince people that it is OK for you to do what you are doing. If you care more about what others will think of you than about what you are doing then you will feel the need to justify yourself.

One way round this is to not explain at all. Don't give any reason but have some stock phrases like 'I don't want to', 'That doesn't work for me' or 'I can't do that'. That, at least, will indicate to you how often you are tempted to give a million reasons for your decision.

And always check your head. Do you feel bad about your decision? If yes – then you are going to be justifying not explaining!

Explain if you like, but don't justify.

25

Managing friendships on social media

Like most things, friendships sometimes need to be managed, especially on social media. Take Facebook for example. You might decide to remove one or more friendships because the exchanges drain you. Then one of them notices and comes back to ask you to explain yourself as she thought the friendship was a good one. What does an empowered woman do? Someone once wrote to me about this very thing. Here is what I replied.

Firstly – you have a right to be friends or not with whomever you like and you don't actually need to justify yourself at all (see the previous Tip).

But maybe she is genuinely interested in some feedback? In which case, I would respond by saying something like this: 'Hi W, yes you are right, I did take you off my friends list some time ago. Every now and again I look at my list and make a decision to only keep on it the people who energise me and where I feel nourished by the connection. I don't think we have that connection any more and I don't think this is good for either of us. So I decided that it was better to remove you from my friends list while sending you from my heart, love and good wishes for your happiness and success. I continue to wish you well for the future.'

Choose online friendships that energise you.

26

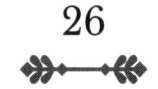

It's OK for people to not like you

Girls are brought up to be people pleasers. We are rewarded for being pretty, and quiet and good and the reward is that people like us. So we learn to suppress our own needs and desires and always put the needs of others before our own.

Hopefully, we start to learn that this isn't doing us any good – emotionally or psychologically – and we begin to reclaim the power in us that has been lying dormant. One of the results of this is that people won't like us because we're not at their beck and call all the time. We have to get comfortable with not being liked otherwise we get trapped into scurrying back into our "like me, please" mindset and losing ourselves in the process.

The fact is we have no control over what others think of us. We can't *make* any one person think or feel in a particular way about us or anything else for that matter. And we'd never be able to please everyone anyway. But more than that – it's actually none of our business what someone thinks of us. It's their business. It's our job to be the best that we can be in all situations and to think well of ourselves.

When I had pink and purple hair (which I did for 23 years) children would often stare and comment on it. Once a little boy said, 'Your hair is purple.' I replied, 'Yes it is, do you like it?' His mother looked on horrified as he slowly shook his head and said, 'No.' I bent down to him, smiled and said, 'That's absolutely fine because I like it enough for both of us.'

It's *your* job to like you – do it well.

27

There is more than one way to listen

We can listen on three different levels: listening to the *story* in the words, listening to the *feelings* behind the words and listening to find out *what is really going on.*

We love listening at the story level – that's often how we connect as women: sharing our stories. And women are also very good, I think, at picking up on the feelings, and often the feelings are part of the story. But it's at the third level of listening that we can really learn about how a person experiences their world. This is especially true when listening to men who often will not even articulate their feelings.

By listening for what is really going on, we use our hearts and put ourselves in another person's situation with compassion. When people say, 'I felt really heard' they mean that someone listened beyond the obvious and tuned into their deepest desires and concerns. One of the greatest gifts we can give to someone is to really hear them. When we connect with what someone's deepest self is saying, the energy of that connection is extremely powerful and can open up new paths for both parties.

Listen differently to find out what is really going on.

28

Accept and embrace compliments

How many times do you deflect a compliment? Instead of saying a simple thank you we deflect it by saying dismissive things like, 'Oh, this old thing, I've had it for *so* long' or 'I'm not sure it's really my colour…'

If you find it difficult to accept a compliment, it's because you aren't in touch with the truth about yourself – that, at your core, you are pure and magnificent potential. It's the ego that is so concerned with living up to others' expectations and trying to prove your worth. The ego's notion is that we are unworthy until proven otherwise. The essence of our true self is just the opposite. In our true essence we are bright and worthy and magnificent.

Never be afraid of shining your light because you are worried that you will put others in the shadows – quite the opposite – you will light up their way! The world needs your magnificence and there is only you who can bring it.

See your own magnificence and shine it out!

29

Just because you're good at it, doesn't mean you should do it

It's our natural instinct to volunteer for things – especially things that need organising. And women are great organisers. We can see what needs to be done, the best way of doing it, and how it's all going to fit together with everything else going on. So we volunteer so we can get on with it.

The problem with this is that people just get used to us doing it and are happy to let us because it gets them off the hook. Yes, it might be true that we will organise "it" quicker and better, but then others never get the chance to practise *their* organising skills.

On a personal level, you will end up doing way too much and not have any time over for yourself. On a professional level, think very carefully what you volunteer for. Offering to organise a meeting may get you some visibility, but perhaps it also puts you in an admin role when the visibility you need is as a manager and a leader. Maybe you should be volunteering to chair a meeting, not organise it.

Think carefully about what you volunteer for.

30

Rethink how you see success and failure

We all want to be successful. But you have to think about what exactly you mean by success. For instance, is success about *getting* that job or is it about *doing* that job really well?

And while it's a great idea to be clear about the end result we want, it's also a good idea to have many small steps charted (e.g. send off application form; get an interview) so you can feel a sense of achievement and pride when you can stand on one step and have your foot up ready for the next one.

What we have to watch out for though is that many small steps of success means that there are many small steps we might fall off or 'fail' at. We should see everything that happens to us (yes, *everything*) as information to guide our next move. In fact, it would be better if we saw that things happen *for* us not *to* us. And never, ever give up.

**Take delight in your successes,
and see your failures as information.**

31

You're the only expert you'll ever really need

We can all benefit by getting tips from others. This is especially true of our women friends, who are a source of great support to us and give us valuable insights. Then there are those whom we don't know who offer advice, like I am doing right now. Each of these Tips might be useful, or not. Only you can decide that. If it's helpful, great. If not, move on.

Here's why. I used to be a self-development junkie. I read anything and everything on how to be better, how to be better, how to be better… And I trusted everyone else's judgement never thinking for one minute that I might have some wisdom inside me that I should be following. Our internal wisdom filter should examine everything we get from an external source: does this resonate with me? Would this advice be good for me to follow? What does my Best Self have to say about this?

We would do well to spend more time on reflection, meditation, walking – anything that puts us in touch with that best part of ourselves that *knows* – rather than turning to an "expert" to advise us.

Ask your internal wisdom for advice, and listen to the answer.

32

Don't make *their* pain *your* pain

Some people think that being detached means being cold and uncaring. This is not the case. Being detached means that you are able to witness, be compassionate and take the best action with a clear and wise head.

For many women, being compassionate comes easily. We can empathise with people, show them we understand, cry with them and share their pain. The problem with this is that if we get on someone else's emotional wheel with them we can't always give them a helping hand to get off it. A powerful woman knows that entering into someone else's pain doesn't help them or us. We can never really understand anyone else's pain and we shouldn't pretend that we can. Joy is easy to share – pain is unique to each individual.

Compassion enables us to offer love, hope and support without climbing on someone's emotional wheel with them.

Practise compassion with detachment.

33

Change your experience of yourself

Many of us have pretty ingrained patterns of guilt, fear and shame and believe at a deep level that there is something intrinsically wrong with us that needs to be punished. But this isn't the truth: it is just a pattern. And beating ourselves up is simply just another pattern – the ultimate pattern to be broken.

By learning to recognise and break the pattern of criticising and beating ourselves up, the essence of our true self can flow through and create a change in our perception and then, a change in our experience of ourselves.

If we are to be successful in creating new patterns then we need to learn how to let ourselves off the hook, and not criticise or beat ourselves up for our mistakes. It is essential to learn how to do this because if we don't, we could sabotage all the other good work we are doing.

What is doubly difficult is that we are the only ones who can actually do it. We can ask for help; we can read guidelines; we can hear other people's stories; but we are the only ones who can actually let ourselves off the hook. It is a daily, hour-by-hour activity: a continuous process of noticing how we put ourselves down and affirming the truth that we are really OK.

Break the ultimate pattern.

34

Let courage trump fear

Courage is a pre-requisite quality for being a powerful woman. Courage doesn't mean you don't feel fear, it means that what you're standing up for is way more important than your fear. Fear stops us from taking action and not taking action is a big mistake. The less we act, the less we will be seen, the less we will make our mark and have an impact.

We can be afraid for a number of reasons. Afraid that we'll make a mistake, afraid that we'll lose respect, afraid that others will judge us…

Fear is the ego whispering to you, 'Who do you think you are?' and 'What will people think of you?' Smile at your fear and say to your ego, 'Thanks for the warning but you're out of your depth ego. There are places I need to go where there is no admission for you. I don't need you right now.' Then work out exactly what it is that you are afraid of. Sometimes that is enough. Knowing what your fear is means you can tackle it head on and dispel it as groundless.

And if you can't find out exactly what the fear is? Then you can ask yourself, 'What would I do now if I wasn't afraid?' Focus on the action you want to take and bypass your fear entirely. Then let courage take you by the hand and lead you.

Ignore fear and let courage guide you.

35

It's OK to show your vulnerability

Everyone feels vulnerable sometimes. Maybe it's when we're extremely tired, or in a new situation and are very nervous, or we're feeling fragile because of criticism we've had. When we're vulnerable our heart is open and our defences are down. It's OK to let this be seen. You are human. And appearing to be super strong all the time isn't being real or authentic.

Of course it doesn't mean we cry all day and become completely ineffective. But it does mean we express our feelings honestly and ask for understanding and help when we need it. Keeping your heart open allows others to know you better and gives them permission to open their hearts too. Once we drop our barriers of invincibility and invulnerability we connect with people differently. Being vulnerable isn't a permanent state – but it is part of who you are.

Be proud to show your real and authentic self.

36

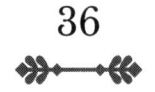

Is a weakness actually a strength?

Many years ago when I was a schoolteacher I went for a promotion that was two grades higher than I was on at the time. I had taught in a number of schools but hadn't done more than a year in any of them. I knew that this would be judged as a weakness in my application. So when someone said in the interview, 'You don't seem to have stayed very long in any one school…?' I replied: 'I wanted to give myself a breadth of experience. I have taught different age ranges, different academic levels, learned about team working from every department I have been in, worked in schools where there were many resources and no resources. I have taught in small schools and in large ones. I can fit into any structure and have contributed – and can contribute – to every team I have been a member of. I have been able to assess my own worth through the variety of classroom situations I have been in and I am excited about this opportunity that I am more than ready for.' I got the job.

So whenever you feel that a potential weakness about you is going to be judged, look for the strength in the weakness, be assured and talk about that. You are here to identify your gifts and share them. Don't hide behind what you see as a weakness.

See your weaknesses as strengths, and present them as such.

37

Don't rush to restore order to chaos

Our tendency as women is to be highly organised and move in to "fix" the situation and restore order. Indeed, if we are managers and leaders we might feel we have a responsibility to do just that. But sometimes we need to step back and see what results from the chaos.

One of the important findings of modern chaos theory is that seeds of order seem to be embedded in chaos, while seeds of chaos are apparently embedded in order. Look up chaos theory and you will see much information and research about the natural order that results from seeming chaos.

Whether our chaotic situation is at home or at work, sometimes stepping back is the best plan. See what develops, see who steps forward, and see what new insights and solutions emerge. Solving the chaos too quickly can put a lid on the creativity and innovation that is right there under the surface waiting to be revealed.

Allow chaos to reveal creativity and innovation.

38

Don't be defensive

It's easy to become defensive when someone gives us negative feedback about our behaviour. This is the time when we might fall into the fight (become the aggressor) or flight (withdraw and become the victim) response. In either of these positions our defences are up and our perception is constricted as we focus on the "wrongdoing" of the other person. And more importantly – our minds and hearts are closed.

It's best to consider someone's feedback as a gift. Consider the feedback gently. Be relaxed about the other person's opinion of you. If the feedback makes you really angry the chances are that there is some truth in it (yes, really). Calm down, let it in, consider what is being said and drop your defences.

Managing our defences helps us to be able to use our intuition more effectively because we stay more connected to our calmer, more whole self. By not being defensive and staying open to the person we can change the dynamic and the energy, and the exchange will contain a seed for something different and out-of-pattern to happen.

Keep the door to your mind and heart open.

39

Not everything worth doing is worth doing well

There are many women who do a piece of work and then fiddle with it, add to it, change bits of it, make it look pretty… All of which is time spent on something that is actually finished instead of moving on to the next thing to be done. The higher up the scale you go at work, the more you are likely to have support whose job it is to lay it out nicely and make it look pretty so we have to learn to focus on what is important not what satisfies our innate desire for creating a pleasing appearance.

We even do this when looking at our careers. We feel we have to do one job perfectly before we can think of seeking the next rung up the ladder. Ambitious men think differently. In mapping out a career path, men work at their present job while keeping an eye on what they need to do for the next one. In contrast, some women become obsessed with perfect standards and then are overtaken when it comes to promotion.

Stop aiming for perfection – just do it and move on.

40

Put yourself first sometimes

Women are so used to putting everybody else first and so good at catering for everyone else's needs, we forget about ourselves. Sometimes it's not a bad thing to say: 'You know what? This is me time.' And let everybody know that this is your time.

Here's a poem by Natasha Josefowitz from her book *Is This Where I Was Going?*

> *TV?*
>
> *Sometimes in the evening*
> *I'm so tired I can't read*
> *I can't write*
> *I can't talk*
> *I can't think*
> *and it's too early to go to sleep*
> *so I watch TV*
> *sitting in bed*
> *but I still feel guilty*
> *that I'm not being constructive*
> *whatever that is.*
> *But where is it written*
> *that it's not okay to waste time?*
> *And anyway,*
> *what's wasted time?*
> *If I enjoy it,*
> *then it's not wasted.*

We need to remember that. Let's just sit in front of the television for an hour if that's what we need to do to relax – without thinking, 'I really ought to be doing this or that', when what we should be doing now is sitting watching television with a cup of tea. That's exactly what we need to do – and it's absolutely fine.

Do whatever your like in your time: your time, your choice.

41

Don't keep quiet about what you want

Many women do this at home as well as at work. At home we expect that our partner should just *know* what we want (based on past experience) or pick up the hints and non-verbal signals we give. They don't. Far better to state clearly what we want and need and open up the discussion.

At work, it's even more important. You are responsible for your own career – no one else. You have to plan it and you have to let the people who can help you know what your plan is. Waiting to see what the organisation has in mind for you won't get you to where you want to go.

I heard a woman CEO of a bank say that (on her way up) she was waiting and waiting for the right promotion to come up. Eventually, she told her boss that she wanted to head the bank in an overseas location. He had no idea she was even interested in that. Within 18 months she had her appointment. Once people know what you want they start to see you in a new framework. Don't make them play guessing games. It's your job, it's your career, and it's your life. Seize it.

Tell your manager what you want.

42

Turn negatives into positives

When we are stuck and dealing with a crisis (maybe we just lost our job) we can be sucked down into a cave of despair. It's hard to breathe here never mind move on. But think back to difficult times in the past when something seemed like a disaster and some time later you had the realisation that if *that* hadn't happened then *this* wouldn't have happened and you wouldn't be where you are now.

Hindsight is a wonderful thing. If only we could see the gift sooner. Finding the gift, even in very difficult situations, is the very thing that can help us to move on.

Things happen *for* us not *to* us. Start to look for the gift in your challenging situation. What are you being asked to step up to? And trust that there is a gift; that everything is in perfect order; that you are in the right place and you're right on time. Finding the gift is your way out of the cave.

See the gift in every situation.

43

Everyone is responsible for running a smooth household

A family is a small community and for it to run smoothly everyone has to contribute. And children need to be involved in family contribution. Of course there are ways children are unable to contribute but there are plenty of ways they can.

One way in which everybody contributed in our house was to do with the weekly shopping. And while the girls couldn't do the shopping all by themselves, it was important that they take a share in it.

So I created a master list of everything that we usually have in stock and I divided the list into areas. Whoever was responsible for doing that part of the list (e.g. tinned goods) would look in the cupboard, see there was only one tin of chopped tomatoes, check the master list, which would say there should be four, and therefore know to write three tins of chopped tomatoes on the list.

What happened very quickly was that they started to do for their area what I was able to do: open the cupboard, quickly look in and see what was missing, and write it down. When we were all doing it, it didn't take very long for everyone to do their section and although it meant the shopping list was done in different handwritings, who cared? I was only doing a fraction of what I used to do and *everyone* was taking some responsibility.

Give your children some responsibility, and lessen your load.

44

Which qualities are you wearing today?

I'm often asked whether I give tips about how women should dress and the short answer is no. I would agree that there are fairly commonly held standards of professional dress for men and women, which would mean your clothes are clean, well-fitting and decent – most people would agree with this, I think – the rest is down to personal opinion.

There are no "shoulds". I once saw a report, which said that women who didn't wear make up wouldn't get on. Rubbish! I meet many senior women who don't wear make up. And what about high heels? And what about trousers vs. skirts? It's all personal preference. And it's all about being authentic. Personally I don't wear skirts – ever. So for me to put on a skirt at work because that fits in with someone else's idea about how I should dress would require me to be inauthentic. Draw attention to your performance not to your physical appearance.

I was saddened to hear once that when asked what one tip she had for women, a female CEO of a large company said, 'Keep your jewellery simple.' I wish she had said, 'Never compromise your personal values.' Or, 'Speak the truth even when others don't.' Or, 'Remember that inner beauty is way more important than outer beauty.' What a wasted opportunity to give the women of that company an inspirational message about how they should *be* not about how they should *look*.

It's true that when we look good, we feel good. But that only lasts as long as the make up. The reverse is more powerful and lasts longer: when we feel good, we look good. And the quickest route to feeling good is by accessing our powerful, authentic selves.

So dress up inside, with courage, with honesty, with compassion, and know that when those qualities shine through you, no one will be interested in your shoes or your make up.

Pay attention to how you dress – on the inside.

45

The balance you *can* achieve

No, I don't mean home/work balance because every working woman knows that this kind of balance is impossible. It has a kind of mythical status – an ideal that makes us sigh when we think about it and stress when we think we haven't got it.

We can't achieve balance relating to home and work: we can compromise. It's like being in the middle of a seesaw: sometimes it dips at one end so we need to move to the other end so we don't fall. Then it dips at the other end so we need to take a few steps back in the other direction. It's *compromise* that means that we can keep adjusting and readjusting according to the priorities of the day – sometimes of the hour!

But the balance we *can* seek and achieve is inner balance. Inner balance means that we have the sureness and confidence to deal with any situation that arises; that we have the inner strength to do what needs to be done; that we never allow our pressures to define us; that we have the presence of mind to always remember that while we can't always control external circumstances we have the ultimate power to choose how we react to those circumstances. This is real power and realising this power ensures that we always remain in inner balance.

So forget about home/work balance. Seek inner balance and know that when you have it, then your home/work integration will be so much more effective.

Seek inner balance for maximum effectiveness.

46

Make time for appreciation and gratitude

Sometimes we think that once we are happy we will be thankful and grateful. In fact, that's the wrong way round. The route to happiness is *through* appreciation. Staying in appreciation keeps our heart open. (Our head is constantly in action – we don't need to worry about that.)

And when our heart is open, we are closest to our inner self, our best self, our authenticity. Powerful women work from their authentic selves so we need to keep the door to that self open so we have constant access to it. Being in a state of gratitude is one of the keys to open that door.

So here is a simple practice to begin your day. When you wake in the morning let your first thought be, 'Thank you for this day; thank you for my life.' And move into your day with an open, joyful heart.

Start the day with simple appreciation.

47

You are more powerful than you know

When we think about power we usually think about how we can get it. We assume we are in a position of powerlessness and so we need to work out how we can acquire the power we think we want and need. In fact, what you need to remember is that you are *already* powerful. You have an immense power inside you. You were born with it. You have the wisdom of generations of wise women inside you.

Unfortunately, many girls and women have grown up with messages – subtle and not so subtle – that we are really not worth much or indeed worthy of success or even of love. So the innate power inside us has been covered over with negative messages and beliefs.

How can we be in balance when this inner conflict is present all the time: the conflict between our real, authentic, powerful self and the self that has been moulded by others? We need to remember who we really are and each time we do this we scrape a bit more mould off that covering and reveal a little more of the preciousness and the power that is our birthright.

So repeat to yourself at regular intervals during the day: 'I *am* powerful and I *will* be seen in the world.'

Embrace your power and bring it to life.

48

Question the voice that says 'I'm not ready yet'

Because you are so brilliant and have such high standards, you see every way that you could be more qualified. You notice every part of your idea that is not perfected yet. While you are waiting to be ready, gathering more experience and sitting on your ideas, other folk are being appointed industry visionaries, getting raises, and seeing their ideas come to life in the world. They are no more ready than you – and perhaps less so.

Research seems to show that men get appointed on potential and women on experience. If this is true, you'll have to work that bit harder to get to where you want to be. So go for the experience you need. Believe in your own potential and go for what you want. There will always be a reason to think that you're not ready. Meanwhile there are 99 reasons for why you are. Start to focus on them.

You are ready now!

49

Dealing with advice

One of the challenges for women as they move up the ladder is that they are expected to take risks and be innovative. And they are expected to take advice from their (often male) managers. It's hard to do both. And what about all the other people who think they know better than you?

Most brilliant women are humble and open to guidance. We want to gather feedback and advice. But here are four things to bear in mind about feedback:

1. Some people won't understand what you are up to (often because you are saying something new and ahead of your time).
2. Some people won't like you.
3. Some people will feel threatened by you.
4. Some people will want to do with your idea only what is interesting or helpful to them.

So interpret feedback carefully. Test advice and evaluate the results rather than following it wholesale.

Listen to advice – but don't always follow it.

50

Update your support network

When we are busy with a demanding job, demanding children, demanding parents and a partner we really want to spend time with… it can be impossible to think we can squeeze in anyone else.

But our support network is invaluable. We feed off them. They sustain us. Here are the kinds of people we need in our support networks:

- People who make us laugh
- People who will just listen to us (not advise)
- People who we always feel better for seeing
- People we can discuss our ideas with
- People whose advice and guidance we trust
- People who will remind us how brilliant we are
- People we can watch a movie with

Check the people in your life and see how many of these needs are being met. It may be that one or two people can meet multiple needs – lucky you then! And remember we don't always have to physically see people. Some of the most important people in my network are women I see only once or twice a year. But just getting an email from them or having a quick Skype is enough to lift me and reenergise me.

Take a hard look at whom you are spending time with (whether offline or online). Are they energising you or draining you? Regular pruning is a good thing to keep us in good shape, healthy and happy.

Make sure your support network is really working for you.

51

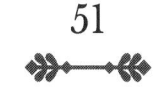

Take a moment to take stock

We live our lives on many lines – family, work, hobbies, extended family, community, volunteer work, exercise groups and on and on. Sometimes we think that balance is about making sure that one of these lines e.g. work, isn't stretching out way further than the others. We try to make sure we are spending time on each of our lines.

The problem with living on the lines is that we are constantly trying to achieve things, to fix things, to plan things. Suppose we looked at living between the lines of our lives? This beautiful poem, *Clearing* by Martha Postlewaite, explores that concept.

Do not try to save
the whole world
or do anything grandiose.
Instead, create
a clearing
in the dense forest
of your life
and wait there
patiently,
until the song
that is your life
falls into your own cupped hands
and you recognise and greet it.
Only then will you know
how to give yourself
to this world
so worthy of rescue.

There is time. Your presence is between the lines. Be patient and settle into your presence and allow it to seep into every fibre of your being. Let 'the song that is your life' reveal itself to you. Step off the lines of your life into the spaces between them. Then you will realise the link between your presence and your power. Your life will be transformed, as will the lives of everyone in it.

Live between the lines of your life.

52

Are you happy with who you are?

As you get used to sensing your own power and realising the value you have for your family, your organisation and your community, you will find that you can trust yourself more and more.

So what are you trusting exactly? You are trusting your own integrity. You are trusting that you know the right thing to do in any situation. You are trusting that you will have the courage to do this right thing. You are trusting that you have amazing inner resources that you can draw on at any time. You are trusting that you are always doing the best you can and that this is good enough.

So make sure every day you look into the mirror, not to check your hair, but to look deep into your eyes and ask yourself:

- *Am I happy with who I am?*
- *Am I happy with the image I project?*
- *Am I happy with my decisions?*
- *Am I happy with how I am living my life?*
- *Am I happy that I am being a great role model?*

Even taking just one of these questions each day, asking yourself honestly and listening for the truth coming from you – for truth will most certainly come – can help you to monitor yourself and guide you back onto your powerful woman path should you stray.

**Look yourself in the eyes every day
and be happy with what you see.**

53

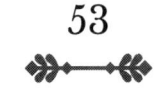

Focus on what you *have* done

I don't know a woman who hasn't made a To Do list into an art form. We plan endlessly to ensure the smooth running of the house combined with our work; we organise family occasions whether it's an 80th birthday party or a family holiday; we write sticky notes and reminders to ourselves to make sure that nothing gets forgotten; we prepare meticulously for meetings to avoid criticism of incompetence, and prepare ourselves emotionally to deal with possible rejection and even hostility. And if everything doesn't run smoothly then at least we can prevent a nervous breakdown!

We all know about goal-setting now and plotting a career path to provide direction for us as we forge ahead. There is nothing wrong with To Do lists or goal-setting but what we have to watch out for is beating ourselves up for all the things we didn't do. We forgot to send the money to school for the school photograph; we forgot to invite someone to the 80th birthday party; we forgot to distribute the agenda before the meeting… Any one of these things can key right into our sense of not being good enough and knock our confidence.

So here's a suggestion. As you write your To Do list for tomorrow, do another list of all the things you have done well *today*. Include everything from work and home:

- Finished that report
- Talked to one of team for 10 minutes about what was troubling her
- Phoned my mother to see how she was

- Offered someone a lift home
- Suggested a new way of doing something to my manager
- Explained to one of my children the importance of telling the truth

It's likely that all these things we are doing are part and parcel of how we live our lives. We don't give ourselves credit for them because they don't appear on our radar. The things that appear on our radar are things that have gone wrong. We have to change this!

Start noticing all the things you're doing right and give yourself due credit.

54

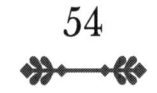

Be aware of hidden opportunities

I've heard people say, 'I haven't been lucky; I just haven't had the opportunities.' But there are some people who wouldn't recognise an opportunity if it stood in front of them and said hello. And there are others who would see the opportunity but not have the courage to seize it.

Some opportunities are easy to spot – the promotion posting, the relocation opening. And some we might dismiss as not being important enough for us to consider. We are asked to attend a meeting at the last minute, or asked to deliver a message to a Senior Executive. It just might be that the very meeting we didn't want to go to is the one where we make a contribution that gets noticed by someone important. And that message we had to deliver gave us the chance to talk to a senior person we wouldn't have had access to otherwise.

I once heard a Senior Partner from Deloitte talking about meeting a Senior Executive, when she was a Junior, at an airport, who he had vaguely known through her activities on the social committee. He found out she was planning to leave and after the conversation went back to Deloitte and negotiated bringing her back as a Senior Executive.

We just never know which conversation is going to be a really important one, or which seemingly menial task gives us access to an important contact. Opportunities surround us all the time. Don't dismiss them out of hand.

Treat all opportunities with respect.

55

The connection between passion and persuasion

Of course you must be passionate about what you do. You must believe in it and speak with enthusiasm about it. This is the only way to be authentic. People will see right through it, and you, if you are only pretending to be passionate. It's your passion and enthusiasm that will excite people and make them want to join you and to follow you.

But while your passion will be important in inspiring people, there's another skill you have to use too – the skill of persuasion. Not everyone will share your passion and to take people with you, you will have to persuade them of the benefits of whatever it is you are suggesting.

You have to be able to explain why this is important for *them*. Not everyone will be able to stand in your shoes, but as a manager and leader you must be able to stand in theirs. Remember to look at the whole thing from their point of view. What are their fears? Why might they be resistant? What's in it for them? Your passion alone will go a long way but it's your persuasion that will win the day.

Be passionate *and* take people with you.

56

Sometimes it's good to rock the boat

When we first take on a new job or role it's prudent to wait and assess what's going on so we can decide what we might want to suggest or change. The problem is that we can get too comfortable with the status quo and too fearful about rocking the boat.

You have things to offer that others don't. That's why you got the job! You are a fresh pair of eyes. You have a responsibility to speak out and make changes if necessary. So never be afraid of being feisty and standing up to people who are trying to obstruct you or keep you quiet. Organisations don't need clones who all think the same way. If there are two people on a board, or on a team, who think exactly the same way then you don't need one of them!

Don't be afraid to be feisty and rock the boat. It might be exactly what's needed. And from the sparks might come great creativity and innovation.

Let your power be seen.

57

Reject the myth that women aren't good at networking

Women are *great* at networking. When we move house to a new area we find out, in a flash, the best schools, the best supermarket, bakery, dry cleaners, child minders, butchers... Why? Because we need to know these things in order to organise our lives.

Unfortunately, some women see networking at work in a completely different light and are reluctant to interact with people, especially if they are more senior. There is only one difference between networking at home and networking at work. At home we need to find out information and we use our interpersonal skills to find it. At work it isn't just about finding out information: it's about an exchange. So we can easily find out who are the people we need to make an impression on, which committee is the best to serve on, which function we really should attend – that's just information and the ability to find it is in our DNA.

What then? Then we need to offer something. The first rule of networking is: 'Give what you've got and you'll get what you need.' Offer something to the people you want to network with – a particular skill, your time, a contact, an idea, an article – this is how you build the relationship. Networking is all about establishing relationships and women's interpersonal skills mean we are excellent at this too. So don't believe the myth that women aren't good at networking. It's just not true!

Take your networking skills to work.

58

It's time to give yourself a break

A friend of mine, Samina Khan, wrote this and gave me permission to share it with you.

It's time.
Time to lay down your weary burden of self-doubt, shame and blame;
Time to stop pushing and driving yourself, forever in search of approval, ok-ness, your own self-worth.
Hasn't it been long enough already for you to know that it's impossible to find something that was never lost in the first place?
Aren't you exhausted enough, spent enough, just plain had enough?
So it's time – just stop.
Stop long enough to feel your heart beat, to feel your breath be the waves of your ocean.
Stop and connect to your own precious self.
It's time to reclaim the lost one inside, the one you've neglected, criticised, abused and trodden on.
It's time to begin again.
Now.
This moment.
It's time.

Take a breath and start again today and remember just how magnificent you are. You just forgot for a little while. Clean the slate and start again now. Then start again at the beginning of every new day.

Remember and recognise your self-worth.

59

You are *not* an impostor

This Tip is a continuation of the previous one about remembering your own worth. It specifically addresses a recurring thought that can derail us very easily.

Many years ago a friend asked me, 'What's your greatest fear?' I replied, 'Being found out to be a charlatan, an impostor, a fake. Someone rumbling me and realising I'm not any good after all.' My friend smiled and said, 'And *that* is the greatest fear of 90% of all women.'

In the last 30 years, working with women at all levels, I have found this to be true. We have a self-critical streak that runs through us. We are really hard on ourselves. We set ourselves impossibly high standards. We worry about the 5% we didn't do well instead of the 95% we did brilliantly. This is the impostor syndrome.

I'm here to tell you that you are *not* an impostor – you are the real deal! You are strong and powerful and dynamic, even if you don't feel it sometimes. Whenever you feel the impostor syndrome rising up take a deep breath and say: 'I'm *not* an impostor. I'm real, authentic and powerful. I'm going to remind myself all day just how brilliant I am.'

And then spend the day noting the things you are doing well, the things you are achieving, the ways in which you are an inspiration. The more you do this, the more your impostor syndrome will slink away realising it is not welcome in your life.

Recognise all the ways you are real, authentic and powerful.

60

Countering workplace myths

While it's true that women now have abundant opportunities to make real contributions in the workplace, old ways of thinking about women die slowly.

You need to understand these stereotypes so that they don't stand in your way. Here are some of the most common misconceptions:

- *Women's families will always come before work.*
- *Maternity leave is disruptive.*
- *Women are emotional but not rational. They aren't tough enough to make decisions based on facts.*
- *Women get their jobs because the company had to comply with affirmative action guidelines. And if they don't get their way, women will claim sexual harassment.*

As much as you might feel like shouting at someone about their outdated attitudes, you need to counteract these myths with your actions, your presence, and your commitment.

Here are some things you can do:

Have a great child care system in place with a backup for emergencies. And if you do have an emergency, which means you have to leave work, don't feel guilty! It could happen to anyone – with or without children. Do what you need to do to minimise the disruption to your work. And put in the hours when there is a key deadline or crisis.

Remind people (calmly) that men and women choose to have children but only women's careers are disrupted as a result.
And as the periods of maternity leave are relatively short in a long and successful career, you will be repaying the investment in you a hundredfold. Once organisations set up systems that mean men and women can take absences to climb mountains, do charitable work, write books and work with small businesses, maternity leave will be seen as just one of the absence options. (Yes – I know we're a long way from that, but it's coming!)

Explain your professional decisions rationally and unemotionally.
But do not lose the passion for your work. And in making your decisions, continue to engage the heart as well as the head.

No matter how good you are there will always be those who say you only got the job to make up the numbers. Never argue with these people.
Just demonstrate your worth over and over again. Openly display your commitment to work. And don't just be good – be brilliant! It seems that women must be brilliant while men can get away with being merely good. That's OK as it happens, because you are brilliant! Never forget it.

Prove the stereotypes wrong.

61

Why you need a mentor *and* a sponsor

It's really important for you to have a sponsor as well as a mentor. They serve different purposes but both are invaluable.

A mentor can educate you on the unwritten rules of the company. They can give you honest feedback on your plans and intentions. Some companies have structured mentoring programmes. In others, you must identify your own. Either way, finding and cultivating a mentor, inside or outside of your organisation, should be an early component of your action plan.

A sponsor is someone with a seat at the table of power. They have credibility. They can recommend you for highly visible assignments and promotions. They're in your corner and will remind others about you if they seem to have forgotten. Finding and cultivating a sponsor is a long-term project. It takes time to earn their respect and confidence.

Start to build those relationships now. Who do you want to advise you? Who can you learn from? Who do you want to mentor you? And who do you want as your cheerleader and biggest supporter? Who do you want as your sponsor? Once you have identified them – ask them!

Find a sponsor as well as a mentor.

62

It's your right to ask for what you want

It's important to recognise that you have the right to ask for what you want. Yes – it *is* a personal right we all have. And if you don't *accept* that you have that right, you'll never be able to do it. It doesn't mean demanding what you want. But saying nothing and hoping the other person will realise what you want, without you having to tell them, is not a good strategy.

Asking for what you want begins a discussion that enables you to find out what the other person wants too, and whether this is in harmony or conflict with what *you* want. Now you have a basis for negotiation. Too many women keep quiet about what they really want and suffer in silence and resentment as a result. Of course it doesn't mean that you will always *get* what you want but at least what you want will be in the conversation.

It's a great lesson to teach children too. Teach them that they can ask for anything at all – provided they accept that the answer might be no. Let's not have the next generation of children (especially girls) being too afraid to speak up about what is important to them.

Accept it's your right to ask for you what you want and speak up about what's important to you.

63

Comparisons kill confidence

Maintaining your self-esteem and confidence is crucial. And there's nothing more damaging to confidence than comparing yourself with other women. We all have times when we think that every other woman is thinner, better dressed, smarter or more accomplished. We worry that all those other women are more qualified for a promotion or career change. And it seems that we never really recovered from our teenage days when we thought that we were the only ones without the cool shoes or the right hairstyle.

Self-doubt is human, but it doesn't define your life or your potential. Take comfort in knowing that all women experience – and can grow beyond – confidence shortfalls and all phases of uncool shoes. You are unique. You have a complete package of qualities and experience that no one else has.

Stop looking at other women and seeing all the areas where you think you are lacking and start looking at yourself and where you are strong. Your job is to shine and you can't do that if you are hiding behind other women who you think are "better" than you.

Stop comparing – start shining.

64

Don't deflect credit for *your* hard work

On the whole, women are very good at being team players. And even when they are the leader of the team, they are quick to credit the whole team for a job well done. There is nothing wrong with this, except sometimes the credit *does* belong to you as the leader. Men accept credit very well – women deflect it and give it to someone else or a group.

Imagine the scenario. You do a great job; you finish an important project on time and within budget; you do a great presentation to your team at which your manager is present... You will be familiar with many such successes. But it's not your performance that's in question here. It's about how you respond to your success. Do you recognise any of these statements?

- *Well I had a lot of help.*
- *I have a wonderful team.*
- *I was lucky that everything just fell into place.*
- *Really, the credit belongs to X.*
- *It was all due to X's input really.*

No! No! No! Firstly, it has nothing to do with luck! You have got to where you are by hard work, determination and more than a few flashes of brilliance. Secondly, don't give away the credit that rightly belongs to you. It's one thing to acknowledge others – it's quite another to put yourself into the shadows completely.

Here are three things to remember:
1. Yes it's good to use we but it's also good, and important, to use I.

2. If you get praised, the *first* thing to say is, 'Thank you. I worked hard on that and I'm really happy with the outcome.'
3. If you want to acknowledge others, do so *after* you've accepted your own credit and say, 'I really appreciate the great feedback and I will pass on to my team how well our work was received.'

Take the credit for your own great work.

65

Equal treatment doesn't mean same treatment

We all know that it's really important to motivate your team and now, more than ever, we realise the importance of treating people equally. However, treating people equally doesn't mean treating them the same. Nor does it mean abiding by the rule 'treat others as you wish to be treated'. This only works if everyone is like you!

Instead of treating people the way you want to be treated, treat them the way *they* want to be treated. Let's take the issue of motivating your team. Some people appreciate constant attention, and others want to be given the task and set off on their own. As the leader, you have to look at the big picture, and some team members may need to get a peek of it too in order to perform at a high level. Others perform at a high level when the dangling carrot is perhaps being named employee of the month. It's the same with rewards. It's no good giving every member of your team a bottle of wine without finding out first if everyone drinks alcohol.

It's your job to work out what motivates your team members and it's also your job to give people the appropriate reward for a job well done. Yes, treat people equally, but you also need to take account of individual need and desires. That's what powerful leaders do.

Take the time to get to know your team.

66

The fine line between comfortable and complacent

It's important not to get too comfortable in your current role. If you are in a role that you know you do well and that your manager is used to seeing you in, there is a danger that not only might you become complacent but your manager might also have a restricted view of you. Your manager can see what you can do, but you also want your manager to see what is possible.

Are you sure that your manager realises your potential? You have to take charge of how you want your manager to see you. And you have to make sure that you are not resting on your comfort level and being fearful of moving *out* of your comfort zone.

You have the power to change how your manager sees you, and the power to direct your own career. *That's* the power you need to access and use.

Be prepared to move out of your comfort zone – and do it.

67

Don't give away your personal power

You might not *feel* powerful and you might not be in a position of power at work, but you actually have access to a lot of personal power. The problem is that we give this power away far too easily.

We give it away when we agree to do something we really don't want to do, but don't know how to say no. We give it away when we react instead of reflecting then responding, thus allowing another person to be in charge of our behaviour. We give it away when we focus on something that happened in the past and spend way too much time thinking about it and getting upset about it. We don't have access to our power, or our energy when we have left it back in the past.

Make a decision today that you are going to:

1. Stop agreeing to things you don't want to do.
2. Respond in your time, in your way, rather than reacting in the moment.
3. Leave the past in the past and focus on now and the future.

Access your power – and make sure you keep hold of it.

68

You can use your power without abusing your power

You need to realise that using your power is not the same as abusing your power. As women we are often afraid of abusing our position power, so we don't use our position power at all and end up doing everything ourselves!

There are two things we need to do here.

Get comfortable with position power.
Unless we do this we're never going to get into the next position. Remember using your position power is different from abusing your position power. And it's part of your job to empower others. So give them the opportunity to shine – you can't do that if you are doing everything yourself.

Learn to delegate.
At home as well as at work! The higher you go the more you need to delegate. And when you delegate, give people the standards you expect and then let them do it.

Embrace your position power – and use it.

69

What's love got to do with it?

The word love, when used in a work context, often makes people nervous. Yet there are many ways at work that we can, and do, show love: showing concern for someone; saying thank you; spending time listening to someone; getting someone a coffee. It is helpful to remember that operating from love simply means making the decision to see what is good and positive and life-giving.

In my experience, many people in the workplace are ready to acknowledge the power of love and how it works because they are sick of hate, conflict and hostility. When we choose the perspective of love, we engage new patterns of acceptance while our work environments become more naturally inclined towards respectful encounters.

Five ways to try embracing love at work:
1. Consciously use the word love five times each day at work.
2. Do three things each day that would be an example of showing love in the workplace.
3. When you hear the word hate, say a sentence using the word love.
4. When a person irritates you, immediately think of one thing you love about them and focus on that – see if your irritation lessens.
5. If you can't get beyond your irritation, look at what the fear is underneath it. What are you afraid of here? Suppose you dropped the fear – now there is nothing for your irritation to hang on.

Operate from love – even at work.

70

Developing your personal power is a lifetime's work

I am often asked for quick tips on developing personal power. Unfortunately, there aren't any. Developing personal power is a lifetime's work. But there are things you could do to make it easier.

Become aware of your thoughts.
Notice your thoughts and notice any patterns in them. A good way to do this is through mindfulness, which means being aware of what is happening *right now*. So if you have a thought about a past argument you might become aware that 'that's the third time I've had that thought today'. You can't start to alter your thought patterns without becoming aware of what they are.

Recognise unhelpful thoughts.
Once you notice your thoughts, decide which are *not* helpful. Thoughts like, 'I'm not good enough' and, 'I'll never be as good as X.' Instead of focusing on them write down the *opposite* of them and read the list every morning and every night.

Remember that self-awareness is the key to your career.
Your responsibility to yourself is to become more self-aware. Especially of the things that block you. Remember that you're not your role, your successes or your failures. You are a being who has come here to shine your essence. So you have to *believe* in your own magnificence.

Do your work. Be magnificent.

71

Goals are good; intent is better

From an early age most of us are taught the importance of setting goals and establishing specific plans for achieving them. This is good advice. The problem is that we become caught up in our goals, and lose our inspiration, meaning and purpose behind what we do. We begin to get lost in the constant struggle to achieve our goals and get incredibly attached to specific outcomes.

Having a clear statement of intent is making a declaration from our deepest and most authentic self as to what our purpose is really about. This can be a simple statement or a few lines from a poem or book. But it is something that deeply represents to us who we are at our core, and how we want to live as a result of this knowing.

You could begin your statement with 'I want to be…' as a start.

- *I want to be kind and compassionate in every interaction.*
- *I want to be an inspiration to others.*
- *I want to be encouraging of others in reaching their full potential.*

Once we have a statement of intent about how we want to be – how we want to show up – we can then use it to stop ourselves getting lost. We can stay in touch with the reasons behind what we are doing on a day-to-day basis. A statement of intent acts as a compass letting us know where to make corrections and adjustments in our behaviour and our decisions, and when we are off course we can bring ourselves back without engaging in self-judgement or blame.

Be guided by your statement of intent: not your goal.

72

A better way to approach presentations

We all get nerves from time to time, and if we let them get the better of us presentations can become something that we dread. But instead of spending a lot of time trying to suppress your nerves, why not see those butterflies that you feel in your stomach as indicating excitement? This is your energy: your excitement and your passion bubbling up which is what you are going to share. Speak from this place – it is the place of your authenticity, and your power.

Remember that the most important thing is that you have to come across in your presentation as being passionate about the subject. If you just talk to slides then really you might as well just give a copy of them to people to read – it wouldn't need you there.

When you give a presentation it's the time to inspire people, to fire them up about this subject. Enthusiasm is infectious. You are there in front of them and they need to see and feel your energy and your passion. So use these nervous feelings – tap into the well of personal power where these feelings live – and share yourself with your audience.

Replace nervousness with excitement before a presentation.

73

You have the power to change your life

I knew a young woman who had been through some very low patches, for some years. She was outwardly popular, building a business, very funny and witty to be with and yet deeply unhappy with her life. She couldn't find the relationship she wanted, she didn't like how she looked, and she was angry most of the time. She saw many things as the causes of her misery – her parents and upbringing, how others had treated her – all external forces.

Then one day all that changed: she was transformed! She felt great; she was happy; her misery had lifted. I asked what had happened. She said she woke up one day and said to herself, 'I am absolutely sick of being miserable and unhappy. This is going to change today. Right now.' Since then her business has gone from strength to strength and she is losing weight. But most importantly, she has stepped into the magnificence that was always there. She was just too invested in blaming things outside of herself to allow herself to *feel* the magnificence.

The point is that we *do* have the power to change our lives but we have to change our minds and our attitudes first. We have to realise that our happiness is in our hands – not anyone else's. Once we have recognised and released that power in ourselves, we'll have the courage to change the circumstances that are damaging to us. And even if our outward circumstances remain the same, how we *live* them will now be different. We'll have a different experience of living.

Change your mind, change your attitude: change your life.

74

One size doesn't fit all

Women today don't want to be like men. We want to be individual and we want to stand out. Yet in many workplaces, conformity is expected. Organisations say, 'We want you to think outside of the box.' But try sticking your neck out…

The good news – if you work with lots of men – is that it's not hard to stand out. If you are in the minority, people have few women to compare you with so it could be argued that it's easier to blaze your own trail. And if you work with lots of women? A woman once asked me, 'I work with amazing, talented, great women. How am I going to stand out without putting in more hours than they do and sacrificing my family?'

You have to remember that it's not the hours you put in or the skills you have which will make the difference. It's *you* – your essence; your presence; the way you speak; the way you treat people; how you handle problems; how you inspire people. It's how *you* put everything together and present *yourself*.

Your personal power is where your authenticity lies. It's where your deep-seated belief in yourself lives. It's where you *feel* your personal worth. No one – *no one* – is like you. And it's your unique combination of gifts, skills, abilities and expression that will make you stand out. The world needs the magnificent being that you are. Don't reduce yourself to how many hours you work: recognise and appreciate your uniqueness.

Celebrate your individuality.

75

The only time to consider what you wear

Don't underestimate the importance of planning for your success. And don't wait to see what the organisation has in mind for you. *You* decide what you want your next move to be and then make sure that you start to acquire the skills you will need. And part of that is to make sure that you dress for your next role.

As a general rule I am very reluctant to advise women on what they should wear and whether to wear make up etc. but there is one point I think is important: if you want your manager to be able to visualise in the next role, then don't make them work too hard. At the moment, maybe you dress very casually – maybe all your team do – but look how the managers and leaders are dressed. Is it different? Are they smarter?

An easy way of helping someone to visualise you in your next role is by dressing and carrying yourself *as if you were already in the role*. Your manager needs to imagine you at the next level – whether it's attending meetings with more senior people, or presenting to them. If they can't visualise you in the role it might make them less willing to sponsor your promotion.

Dress for the job you want, not the job you have.

76

It's not just about the job

Once you have an idea about the next job you want, you need to weigh up very carefully what's going to be involved.

Might you have to relocate? How will the family feel about that? Will you be expected to work longer hours? To work weekends? Do you have extra childcare support on hand? How do you handle stress? Will you be able to sleep at night? What about the peers you are leaving behind and who you have been promoted over – how will you handle those relationships? How will you deal with comments that you only got the promotion because you're a woman? Who will your next manager be? Are you happy about that?

You will notice that all these questions are nothing to do with the job itself. But they are issues you will have to consider carefully. Some women may choose not to go for that next promotion. They love their current job and they have a life outside of work that they also love. Success for them is being fulfilled in all the areas of their lives and not having to compromise on any one of them. But if your career is where your heart is make sure you consider *all* the aspects then you are well and truly prepared for your success.

Consider where your happiness lies as you weigh up your promotion.

77

Your body is your friend

We all know that it's important to exercise, to eat well and to get enough sleep. Sometimes, these seem like a luxury if not downright impossible!

So let's make it easier. Start to pay attention to the signals your body is giving you about what needs attention. Your body is an intelligence system in its own right. Because it's the densest part of you – physical matter – it takes a while for things to register there. For instance, if you are fearful your heart rate might go up. The fear comes first *then* it is registered in the body.

If you start dropping things, maybe your concentration is flagging and you need a 10-minute power nap. If you have a pain across your neck and shoulders, ask yourself what you are stressed about. If you have a stiff neck ask yourself what you are being inflexible about.

Talk to your body. It might sound ridiculous but your body is a tool for you to express your wonderful essence in the world. If it's not working properly it might mean there is a blockage to your personal power being realised. A few years ago I contracted dengue fever when returning from Thailand. Six months later I had a car crash. Both these events left me with no energy and extreme tiredness. I was forced to listen then and ease up! Pity I didn't tune a little earlier to see what was going on. Now I am much kinder to my body and thank it every day for how it's serving me.

Listen to what your body is telling you.

78

The importance of building relationships in your career

As women, we are so good at building relationships – with family, with friends, with people in the community – but when it comes to work we become strangely shy. Maybe we are afraid that we will appear to be falsely friendly. Maybe we don't want it to look like we are building a relationship with someone just for what we can get out of them later. So we remain distant (calling it professional) or we retreat behind electronic communication where we can video conference with people across the world quite happily.

The personal relationship is much undervalued and underestimated. Systems run on the relationships within them. The person-to-person communication is critical whether the other is our manager, a colleague or a supplier. We need to be willing to really get to know people: to look them in the eye, listen to them and really try to understand where they are coming from. Being able to connect with people is a key leadership skill. Make sure you are developing it.

Relationships drive business and underpin success; make sure you develop yours.

79

Being assertive is not being aggressive

There are three ways of behaving: submissive, assertive and aggressive. Both submissive behaviour and aggressive behaviour are characteristic of people who lack confidence not just in their own abilities, but also in themselves as individuals. There is a better way. This is the assertive way.

What assertiveness means.
Getting your needs met without interfering with the rights of others.
Assertive behaviour means that you express your wants, needs, opinions, feelings and beliefs in a direct and honest way. This involves recognising that in any situation you have needs to be met and the other person (or people) have needs to be met; you have rights and they have rights. And the aim is to satisfy the needs and rights of both parties.

What assertiveness looks like.
Stating clearly what you want, need and feel; making brief statements that are to the point; saying no when you want to; giving praise and taking constructive criticism when necessary; finding out the wants, needs and feelings of others; making decisions; standing up for yourself; acknowledging the other person's standpoint; speaking to people as you wish to be spoken to yourself.

Now if you start to do all these things and people aren't used to it – they are used to you being submissive and always doing what others want – then they will think you are being difficult and may well accuse you of being aggressive. But the aggressive way is: demanding, blaming, threatening, giving orders inappropriately, interrupting, attacking, putting others down, forcing others to do things, expressing opinions as facts, making assumptions, using sarcasm. That is not being assertive.

Assertiveness is a skill and it needs practice. Make sure you're not being aggressive, rude or threatening, and make sure you are not agreeing to a load of things you don't want to do. That's a good start to the new assertive you.

**Be clear, calm and direct.
Assertiveness is a skill. Practise it.**

80

Let's practise detachment

Specifically, I'm talking about detachment from the need to get your own way. It really is possible to be passionate about what we're trying to express without being attached to how it's received. When we are attached to what we are saying, and to the need to convince others that we are right, we often end up forcing our ideas on others or distorting our beliefs simply to gain the approval of others.

Basic assertiveness techniques teach us to start by understanding the other person's point of view; then say how we feel; then state our position. As long as we have said everything we needed to say, we can let go of our expectations about the outcome. This is detachment. It gives us the freedom to communicate without the pressure of needing to win the argument.

By being detached we can find peace with however our comments are received and with whatever direction a conversation takes. Who's right and who's wrong becomes irrelevant. Now the door is open to creativity and innovation.

Let go of your attachment to the outcome.

81

A new way of looking at your job

I once read about a man who was a cleaner in a hospital. He cleaned a ward where there were people in comas. He used to change the pictures on the walls and clean them meticulously. Someone asked him why he was so careful about this as the patients couldn't see them anyway. He answered, 'My job is to assist the doctors and nurses in the healing process. When these patients become conscious I want them to be able to see beautiful things on the walls they have to look at.'

He didn't see himself as "just a cleaner". He saw himself as an important part of the healing process in the hospital.

So how do you see *your* job? What important part of the bigger process do you play? How are you making someone else's job easier? How are you adding value to someone else's life? Never see yourself as "just a...". We are all serving a bigger whole and every part is important.

Look at your job and see its real value.

82

Keep your energy high

The best way to access energy is to get it directly from source – the air, the trees, water, the sun. Of course we can get a quick fix from the nearest high energy person and if you are high energy you will recognise the times when people have sought you out to be around you and talk to you and after a while say, 'Thank you so much I feel so much better now!' While you are left feeling completely drained...

You can stop people from taking your energy. This is how you do it. Inside yourself say, 'You know what? You need energy right now and you can have energy, but you are not going to take mine. You can have the energy coming through me.' Open yourself to receive energy and visualise it coming through you to the person sitting in front of you. As you visualise energy coming through you to the other person, they will be energised – as will you, too, by the way – but you won't be drained of your own energy because it's not your energy that they are taking. I do invite you to really have a go at this and see that it works for yourself.

For yourself – use the sources and resources that are around you outside and make sure you spend some part of each day boosting your own energy from nature. We all know that five minutes in the fresh air can make a world of difference. Identify the places where you can go easily to replenish your spirit. You know it makes sense!

Be present with nature at least five minutes every day.

83

The head vs. the heart

The higher up the career ladder we go, the more we are paid to be able to evaluate the parts of a complex situation and make a judgement call followed by a decision. We use our heads to do this and we are fine-tuning our intellectual skills all the time so we can do it quicker. But sometimes we can go round in circles. We swing between 'I'll do this' and 'No, this is better'. We put enormous stress on ourselves especially if we feel there are serious implications for whatever decision we are going to make.

The truth is that the head doesn't always have the answers. Next time you are in this situation try this: write down your issue and write down all the things you have thought of or tried. Also write down the feelings you have been having as you have been struggling with this issue.

Now put your paper down and sit quietly and recreate a feeling of great love – for a person, or a child, or a beautiful scene you saw. It's important that you *feel* the love. Feel it in your heart, feel your heart getting bigger and then feel the love spreading out from your chest to all the parts of your body. Stay still as that feeling of love completely envelops you.

After a couple of minutes, staying in that place of love, pick up your paper look at your issue again and ask yourself, 'What is the least stressful thing I can do in this situation?' Then wait. Then start writing. You may well find that the solutions that present themselves to you are very different from the ones your head came up with. And note your feelings now. Has your stress reduced? This technique is called Freeze Frame and you can find out more about this and other techniques at www.heartmath.com.

The more you practise this, the quicker you will be able to enter into the heart state that can lead to more effective solutions. Try it when making a decision. Try it before a difficult meeting. Try it after a conversation that hasn't gone well. Try it in the middle of a situation that is just about to spiral out of control. The more you practise the more you will be able to do it in the moment.

Let your heart decide sometimes.

84

Acknowledge the truth about yourself

As women, we have had lots of messages about how we should be. The main ones seem to be: be good; be quiet; be pretty, be nice. As little girls we learn quickly that we get rewarded and validated by being any of these things. Conversely, if we are *not* any of these things we can feel very quickly that there is something wrong with us. And as we grow into women we get messages reinforcing this: we should be more feminine, we should make ourselves look more attractive, we shouldn't be authoritative, we should be empathetic. So for most of our lives we have been given *someone else's* ideas about who we should be as women.

This must stop right now! The truth is that at our core we are brave, bold, amazing, creative, powerful beings. We have just covered it over in order to please others. So we say sorry way too much, we don't put ourselves forward etc. Let's remove these blocks.

We're not doing it to *acquire* personal power: we already have power at our core. We are doing it to *release* the power that is within us and do it consciously and with our heads held high.

**The truth about you is that you are magnificent!
Feel it! Be it!**

85

Change your self-talk

How many times a day does something go wrong or you make a mistake and then think, 'Oh I'm so stupid!' or 'I'm useless at that!' Know that every thought you have is making its way into your cells and helping to define you. That's not just some thoughts – that's *every* thought! And by the way that goes for negative thoughts we have about someone else too e.g. 'he's a jerk' when he cuts in front of you in the car. *He* can't hear our thoughts but our brain hears them and calibrates them into *our* DNA.

So, firstly, stop the negative self-talk. And secondly, start to think positive thoughts about yourself all day. And the best way to keep your whole frame of mind positive is to think thoughts of gratitude all day long. What a fabulous sunset, thank you. My daughter is so great, thank you. I love my coffee in the morning, thank you.

My aim with these Tips is to help you to transform how you live your life, and as you do that, you will transform yourself too. Bit by bit, Tip by Tip. Replacing negative thoughts (especially about yourself) with positive ones is something that can become a habit and you *will* transform as surely as the caterpillar becomes the butterfly.

Replace negative thoughts about yourself with thoughts of gratitude.

86

The perfection block

Many of us have a desire to be perfect in everything we do. This is especially true of working mothers. We want to be successful career women *and* great mothers. We feel judged by women who choose to stay home with their children, for neglecting ours. We feel judged by career women who have no children, as not being really committed to work because we ask for flexible working arrangements.

So we aim for perfection. At work, at home, as mothers, as daughters, as friends. Perfection in how we look, perfection in how we manage our time and our lives, perfection in our relationships.

How our perfection block shows up:

- We feel it *before* we apply for a job. In fact it can even *stop* us from applying because we're worried we're not a perfect match
- We feel it once we start the job. We expect to be perfect from day one so we're terrified of making a mistake
- We feel it if we *do* make a mistake. We think people will remember it forever when in reality it's *us* who remembers it forever
- We feel it if we think we need a haircut or we wore the wrong shoes...
- We feel it if our child is sick and we still go to work (even if their Nana is there with them)

Do you think for one minute that men worry about these things? No. They are always just looking for the opening and working out how they can seize the next opportunity.

Perfection is *not* a good goal to have, mainly because it's not achievable! And it's not necessary. No one is perfect. Sometimes we have a bad day at work; sometimes our house is messy; sometimes we snap at our mothers; sometimes we have no patience with our children. We shouldn't be aiming for perfection. We should be aiming for good enough. And remember, while you are aiming for good enough, you are probably being excellent!

A powerful woman is not a perfect woman. A powerful woman is one who accepts that all the parts of ourselves don't always fit neatly together in a beautiful jigsaw. A powerful woman is one who is gentle with herself and reminds herself that she is doing the best she can. A powerful woman is one who can laugh at the mess her life is sometimes. A powerful woman is one who can bring herself back to her centre with a few deep breaths. A powerful woman is one who knows who to call who will remind her how fabulous she is. A powerful woman is not perfect: she is good enough.

Be a powerful woman not a perfect woman.

87

The importance of knowing yourself

The continuing journey to increase self-awareness and know ourselves is critical for leaders. Actually it's critical for everyone. One very senior woman who came on a leadership programme I was running said it was the first time in seven years she had really reflected on herself. Self-reflection *must* be built into your schedule.

So what should you be reflecting on? The main thing is your own life story. Our stories make us who we are. Our lives have taught us many important things but the lessons will be lost if we don't reflect on them.

What is *your* story? What have you learned about yourself? How have you learned it? Who knows all the parts of you? What are your strengths? What needs work? Be real and honest with yourself. Maybe keep a journal to record your thoughts, 10 minutes a day would suffice.

We are used to talking about our tragedies: when we were betrayed, who said what, how we felt when someone criticised us. These aren't the stories I mean. These stories keep us running round on an emotional wheel. The story I want you to reflect on is the story of your life. What helped to shape you? What were you passionate about when you were a child? What did you learn from periods of hardship? Our life stories have shaped what drives us, what motivates us. The source of your power lies within the life you have lived. Find it and use it.

Learn from your life story.

88

How to fail

Advice on how to fail is an odd thing to write about, I know. But the fact is that we are *not* perfect and we will make mistakes along the way. So for a start it's better to banish the concept of failing and replace it with the concept of learning from our mistakes.

The problem we have with making mistakes (and failing) is that we beat ourselves up when we *do* make a mistake and feel bad and guilty. This immediately takes us out of a learning environment and into a self-blame and self-hate one. As if that isn't enough, we then move straight into the "I'm worthless zone", which can paralyse us completely.

Things to remember when you make a mistake:
- Accept that you have made a mistake, admit it and apologise for it
- Do whatever you can to minimise the impact of your mistake and put right whatever you can, even if you have to go a few extra miles to do it
- Evaluate how the mistake happened and put things in place to make sure the same mistake couldn't happen again
- Work out what learning there is in this for you

Notice that none of these steps involves beating yourself up or feeling that you are worthless. These negative thoughts just enable you to leap onto the emotional wheel of self-doubt where you will go round, and round, and round. Best plan? Don't even get on that wheel!

Take the emotion out of failing.

89

Taking risks takes practice

When we have worked hard to get to a particular position, it's great to be comfortable in our level of expertise. The problem is, the more comfortable we are the less risk-averse we are. Yet the higher up the ladder we go the more risks we will have to take! So we need to practise risk taking.

Identify something small you can do.
Replying to a difficult email; giving feedback to someone you know will be defensive; making an unpopular decision. Choose something that won't have terrible consequences if you get it wrong but which you have been putting off. Notice how you feel when you have done it. Your confidence is growing right there. Now set yourself some more risks to take.

Watch out for any negative thinking that stops you.
Thoughts like, 'I'll be seen as ineffective if I don't do this correctly.' And, 'If I mess this up I won't get another chance.' As soon as you notice the thought, think the opposite immediately: 'My track record is good and people know I am effective in my job.' And, 'There's no reason to think I will mess this up and I can take corrective action immediately if it doesn't work out.'

Just switching your thoughts will take the brake off your willingness to take a risk and you can grow your risk-taking muscles instead of hiding behind your fears.

Get comfortable taking risks.

90

Redefining luck

When talking about their successful careers, I hear a lot of women say, 'I was very lucky...'. Lucky that they had the right boss; saw the right job advert; were in the right place, at the right time... As soon as we give the credit to luck, we deny our own qualities of hard work, determination, perseverance, and talent. So let's redefine luck.

See an opportunity.
People who complain that others have all the luck wouldn't recognise an opportunity if it stood in front of them and said hello. To see an opportunity means we are constantly aware of what is going on around us: what's coming to our attention and how things and people are relating to each other. (Here's an extra tip: if something is brought to your attention from two different sources it's a clear message that this is important information for you.)

Have the courage to *act* on the opportunity.
This often involves taking a risk: speaking out about something or going for a promotion that seems out of your league.

We don't fall into things. We cooperate with what is unfolding before us.

Luck = awareness + courage.

So stop telling people you were "just lucky" and start telling them you saw an opportunity and were courageous enough to take it.

> **Banish the word lucky when talking about your achievements.**

91

The 4D approach to household tasks

If we can't pay someone to do our household tasks we need to be able to, at least, reduce them. And if they do need doing then it doesn't always have to be us who does them.

This is the 4D approach to tasks. It's based on three questions.

Does this job need to be done?
For instance, ironing sheets, ironing underwear, ironing socks? If the answer is no, then DROP it. If the answer is yes, this job does need to be done, then proceed to the second question.

Does it have to be done now?
For example, vacuuming? If the answer is no, it doesn't; it could wait until tomorrow, then DELAY it. If the answer is yes, it does need to be done now because I have people coming in half an hour, move on to the third question.

Does it have to be done by me personally?
If the answer is no, it's not me who needs to do it, then DELEGATE it.

If the answer is yes to the third question, then you're onto the fourth D, which is then DO it.

So those are the four Ds: Drop it: Delay it; Delegate it; Do it.

You'll be pleasantly surprised how many things you don't need to do if you apply the three questions to each task.

Reduce your household tasks with the 4D approach.

92

Choose your body language carefully

There is a lot of information now about what you should and should not do regarding body language. I think there are only two questions we have to ask ourselves: 'How does my body language change how I feel?' And, 'What impact is my body language having on others?'

My most comfortable standing position is with my arms crossed but I got feedback that it appeared to be arrogant and domineering. I didn't want to give that impression to people so I stopped standing like that. So get some feedback on your own body language.

I remember when I had to see the headteacher of one of my daughters about something I wasn't happy about. When I get excited about something, I speak quickly, use my hands and lean forward, but this can be very intimidating for the listener who stops listening! I really wanted the headteacher to hear me so I did three things: made sure I could feel the back of the chair against my back throughout (so no leaning forward); placed my hands on my lap and loosely held one thumb (stopped me waving my hands about); lowered my voice *slightly* which meant that in order to concentrate on speaking a little lower I had to slow my speech down. It worked perfectly. We had a great conversation and I got the result I wanted.

It's worth remembering that our body language can actually change how we feel. In a group once, a woman spoke while leaning forward with her head down and her voice almost inaudible. She looked and sounded crushed. I asked her to sit up, cross her legs, put one arm across the back of the chair of the woman next to her, then asked her to carry on with her story. Her voice was different, her tone was different;

she looked and sounded confident. That transformation happened because she changed her body language.

Three things to check when you monitor your body language:
1. What is it I need to convey in this situation?
2. What body language will best help me to convey this and feel confident?
3. What impact is my body language having on others?

Whatever advice you read, whether from me or anyone else, always check it out for yourself. The important thing to remember is that you have a choice about what body language to adopt. Choose well!

Be conscious of your body and make its language work for you.

93

Your relationship with yourself

We all want great relationships in our lives. And having fulfilling relationships starts with the one you have with yourself. You have to become – *to yourself* – your lover, your partner, your best friend. Why is this important? Because your relationship with yourself determines the quality of all other relationships in your life. Being your own best friend enables you to provide positive self-care and a resilience that allows you to navigate the ups and downs of life.

So there are some things to stop doing and some things to start doing. We have to stop criticising ourselves, judging ourselves, beating ourselves up for our mistakes and standing on the platform built of "I am unworthy" bricks. Here are five things to start doing:

1. See everything that happens as happening *for* you and not *to* you.
What information does this have for you? What can you learn from this? If this had happened to your best friend what would you be saying to her now? Say it to yourself.

2. Begin living in the here and now.
Stop reliving every negative life experience you've ever had. They're over. They're gone. Reliving them and talking about them keeps them alive and is taking your energy away from where you need it: here, and now.

3. Take your time!
Stop pressuring yourself. Take delight in little things. Point them out to yourself. Find things to laugh at every day. Let things unfold before you instead of trying to control everything. Be happy on your own.

4. Do one nice thing for yourself every day.
Do this consciously. Whether it's a 5-minute sit down, a great cup of coffee, a new lipstick, using body cream after a shower (yes, you do have time). And as you do it say to yourself, 'I deserve this.' Because you really do!

5. Forgive yourself.
For every mistake you think you made practise forgiveness, and remind yourself that there are no mistakes – only new choices to be made.

Become your own best friend.

94

Are you willing to change?

I see a lot of information around about how we really can't change ourselves. We have a basic personality type and that can't be changed. Or we were born under a certain star sign so we are always going to have certain traits. Or our character is formed around age 7 and we will always carry that with us. Now, while not ignoring the tendencies that we might have from all these things, we have to accept that as adults we do have a choice about how we want to be and we can't hide behind the "it's just the way I am" position.

First we have to decide whether there is anything we *want* to change. And we can only decide that when we have done two things:

1. Regularly engage in honest self-reflection.
How did we feel after that interaction? Why does that irritate me so much? What could I have done or said differently?

2. Get some feedback about your behaviour.
If you are a manager or a leader then this isn't easy as those who work for you may be reluctant to give you negative feedback. If you have a 360° feedback loop this is easier. Find out whether your intention matches the impact you are having.

Once you have done these two things you can decide what you want to change in yourself. Do you need to be more patient? Do you need to stop trying to fix people? Do you need to be more self-sufficient and less needy?

Get a plan.
Adopt some new behaviours (not all at once) and start to put them into

practice until they become a habit (I think six weeks is the optimum time for this). Don't worry if people seem not to notice at first. They might still be running an old story about you. And it might not suit them to see the new you. Just know that you *do* have the power to change but it has to start with the willingness to change. You *can* do it!

If you are willing to change, you *can* change.

95

Warriors offer peace first

Warriors are the voices of empowerment. They are the voices that elevate our spirit with courage, invoke the spirit of the warrior that we all have within us, and lead us out of our apparent darkness, back to light and life. We can be warriors of ourselves, our families, our communities or humanity at large.

What we need to remember is that invoking the warrior, being the warrior, becoming the warrior – none of this needs to be about "war". Martial arts teachers, as well as many spiritual teachers, say, 'The true warrior always offers peace first.'

But the willingness to offer peace can perhaps only come if we have peace within us. And peace within can only come from knowing our true strength, the source(s) of that strength, and how we are going to use that strength for acts of good. We may be strong in body, and even in mind, but a weak heart and spirit invokes the spirit of fear, inaction, the spiral of negativity and every other negative emotion that comes with them.

So yes, be a warrior. But be at peace with yourself first, and be prepared to offer peace to others before going to war with them.

Be a peaceful warrior.

96

The importance of looking after your body

Now of course we all know this – in our heads! – but still we don't do it. We don't get enough sleep, we eat junk food, we drink too much caffeine and alcohol… We all know the things we shouldn't do. What we don't fully appreciate though, is why we should look after our bodies.

The thing is, it isn't just about our bodies. Our bodies are only one piece of the picture. As well as a physical self (our bodies) we have an emotional self, a mental self and a spiritual self. Our bodies are the densest part of us and our spirits are the lightest. Our bodies carry and transmit our feelings, our thoughts and the spiritual principles by which we live. Our body is the vehicle that carries our essence into the world. Our feelings express themselves through a smile or a frown. Our mind expresses its determination by focusing on a strict diet for healing, or a gruelling training schedule for an athlete. Our spirit is seen as a calming presence to those around us.

So we need to keep our bodies clean and vibrant. Yes, we feel good if we look good, so we can pay attention to appearance if we want to. But it isn't just about appearances. Our inner power and beautiful essence is expressed through the tool that is our body. So take care of yours so you can properly live your power.

Your spirit appears through your body – let it shine.

97

The important meeting is the one *before* the meeting

I'm not talking about the usual preparation here: being clear why you are there in the first place, ensuring you have an agenda, preparing the points you want to make, deciding how you will deal with being ignored or interrupted... I'm talking about the meetings you need to have *before* the important meeting that's planned.

You will need to combine your networking skills, your influencing skills and your communication skills to make sure that you have people at that same meeting who know where you are coming from and support what you are going to say. It's worth investing time in these meetings to get people on side. The worse thing you can do is to say something at the important meeting that is completely new to everyone there. Very quickly people will be throwing challenges at you and you will become defensive and having to justify yourself. Often there isn't the time to explain properly the points you want to make and if you are nervous and feeling under pressure the problem will be compounded.

Find your allies and take the time to talk to them beforehand, and listen to them. If you aren't being clear enough – this is the time to find out. Then you can refine your contribution for the *actual* meeting.

Identify your allies before that important meeting.

98

Myths about delegating at home

There are lots of household jobs that don't actually have to be done by you personally *and* there are many reasons why women don't delegate at home. Here are three of them.

It would take me too long to explain. I can do it quicker myself.
This is true – but only because you have had more practice. If others had had as much practice as you, they would be equally good. If you spend a little time now teaching someone else how to do the task, you will save yourself much more time in the long run.

It's my responsibility as mother, or as wife.
If you believe this you are putting unfair pressure on yourself. The adverts we see and stories we read paint a vivid picture of how it is to be the perfect wife, mother or daughter, but you are unlikely to achieve perfection in even one of these roles, never mind them all, so don't even try. If you really feel that it's your responsibility to do these jobs, you are never going to be able to get rid of them. Work on your belief that it's your responsibility.

I've always done them. Everyone expects me to do them.
And you could well be the one to carry on unless you change other people's expectations of what you are prepared to do. Your wellbeing is important, as is your time. Just because you have always done something doesn't mean to say you should have to continue. It won't necessarily be easy to change the habits of a lifetime, but start by asking yourself: why should it always be me?

Accept that it's OK to delegate at home – then do it!

99

How to develop a personal vision

Whatever stage in your career you are at, it's important to have a personal vision about your work and your life against which you can track your journey. When you think about your future career, don't think, 'I'll see what they have in mind for me.' When you think about your life in the future, don't think, 'More of the same really. I'm quite happy.' You have to allow yourself to dream.

Here are five questions to consider:

1. If your life was perfect and your dreams came true, what would your life and work look like in 10-15 years?
2. If you won the lottery tomorrow, how would your work and life change?
3. What do you want your legacy to be after you have died?
4. What would you love to do or experience before you die?
5. If money was no object and you knew you couldn't possibly fail, how would you want to spend your day: what would make you jump out of bed with excitement?

I review my personal vision every six months and would suggest you do too. Your dream might change as you change. But if you don't know where you are headed, you'll never know if you are on the right track.

Allow yourself to dream – then make it a reality.

100

The golden rules for every busy woman

These are my 10 golden rules for every busy woman to live a happy, fulfilled and successful life.

1. I am not on call to all of the people, all of the time.
2. I have needs of my own which might not be the same as my friends, family or colleagues.
3. I don't have to say yes to every request I get.
4. I don't have to carry on doing something just because I've always done it.
5. Time spent relaxing is time well spent.
6. There is no such thing as a perfect wife, perfect mother or perfect child.
7. Time spent feeling guilty could be spent doing more enjoyable things.
8. I shouldn't always do it for them if they are capable of doing it for themselves.
9. I should give myself the same care and consideration that I give to others.
10. I should remember at all times, especially in the face of criticism, difficulties and anxiety, that I am doing the best that I can.

Your powerful life is waiting for you – go and live it!

If you liked this book...

If you enjoyed these Tips then you might also like *Reclaim Your Power, Reclaim Your Life: Living Your Life as a Powerful Woman.* It's full of ways to help you to transform how you live your life and expands on many of the Tips in this book looking at all aspects of your life.

And if you are preparing for, or are in, a leadership position, look out for my book *On the Path to Authentic Leadership,* which will help you to develop a unique leadership identity that acknowledges your gender base while maintaining your credibility.

Praise for the Powerful Woman Tips

'I thoroughly appreciated each and every powerful woman tip. Even though on occasion it didn't address a current circumstance, I was well aware of its value for a future one. Women helping women is the wave of the present and frankly, that thrills me.'
Karen Casey, PhD
Author, Seminar Leader, Speaker
www.womens-spirituality.com

'Pithy, positive and to the point, Geraldine's tips have challenged and encouraged me to step up into a bolder version of myself at work and in life. Let them guide you if you want to see a quantum leap in the quality of your effectiveness, relationships and satisfaction.'
Sile O'Broin
Communication Consultant, UN agencies in Italy

'A great excuse to take a few minutes out to think about what life is all about, recalibrate priorities and set yourself up positively for the day ahead.'
Siobhan Camplisson
Manager, Global Pharmaceutical Company

About the author

Geraldine M Bown is the founder and Managing Director of Domino Perspectives; a former President of the European Women's Management Development Network; a founder member of the European Institute for Managing Diversity; and co-founder of the Diamond Edge Programme for women leaders.

Geraldine has spent over 30 years working in the areas of women's development, diversity and spirituality. She is known for her transformational training and inspirational presentations. She is a past recipient of an ASTD Excellence in Practice citation for her Diversity work with PepsiCo in over 30 countries. Geraldine provides programmes and coaching for empowering women, and leadership programmes and one-on-one executive retreats for men and women in Connemara, Ireland.

She has co-authored three books for women managers translated into over 10 languages; co-authored From Diversity to Unity book and workbook with Mary Casey and authored two sets of Diversity & Inclusion Conversation Cards for leaders and managers.

Personally, Geraldine is a Reiki Master and in September 1998 was ordained as an Interfaith Minister and Spiritual Counsellor. She completed a Postgraduate Certificate in Spiritual Development and Facilitation at the University of Surrey Management School in 2007.

She is also a certified facilitator of SQ21 – the Spiritual Intelligence Assessment Tool. The assessment tool measures 21 skills that combine to create the ability to be wise and compassionate in our behaviours, while maintaining inner and outer peace – even under great stress.

Geraldine lives in the heart of Connemara, Galway in Ireland.

www.powerfulwoman.net
www.dominoperspectives.co.uk
www.interfaithministers.ie
geraldine@powerfulwoman.net

Printed in Great Britain
by Amazon